I Love
Dinosaurs

By Steve Parker
Illustrated by Chris Buzer

First published in 2006 by Miles Kelly Publishing Ltd
Bardfield Centre, Great Bardfield, Essex, CM7 4SL, UK

Copyright © Miles Kelly Publishing Ltd 2006

This edition printed in 2009

4 6 8 10 9 7 5 3

Editorial Director Belinda Gallagher
Art Director Jo Brewer
Junior Designer Candice Bekir
Cover Artworker Stephan Davis
Production Manager Elizabeth Brunwin
Reprographics Stephan Davis

ISBN 978-1-84236-779-7

Printed in China

British Library Cataloguing-in-Publication Data
A catalogue record for this book is available
from the British Library

www.mileskelly.net   info@mileskelly.net

www.factsforprojects.com
The one-stop homework helper —
pictures, facts, videos, projects and more

Contents

Tyrannosaurus rex

One of the biggest hunting animals ever to walk the Earth was *Tyrannosaurus rex.* This huge meat eater had more than 50 teeth. Each one was bigger than your hand.

Even bigger!

For many years, people thought Tyrannosaurus was the biggest meat eater. In fact *Giganotosaurus* was even bigger!

Tyrannosaurus weighed about 7 tonnes – that's as heavy as two elephants.

The big teeth were like sharp saws. They easily sliced through skin.

The arms of Tyrannosaurus were tiny and probably useless.

5

Brachiosaurus

One of the biggest dinosaurs that ever lived was _Brachiosaurus._ It weighed over 50 tonnes – more than a huge truck. It was also one of the tallest dinosaurs. Its head stretched 13 metres above the ground.

Giant feet!

Brachiosaurus had huge feet and made footprints one metre across. Look on a tape measure to see how wide this is.

Brachiosaurus probably spent its whole life eating. Its neck was the same length as a flag pole!

Maiasaura

This big plant-eating dinosaur laid its eggs in a bowl-shaped nest in the ground. *Maiasaura* protected its eggs from hungry hunters. When the baby dinosaurs hatched, they were too small to leave the nest. They needed their mother to bring them food.

Each baby Maiasaura hatched from an egg that was about as big as your two fists placed end-to-end.

Mega eggs!
Some mother dinosaurs laid eggs that were 50 times as big as a hen's egg.

The nest was 2 metres across and contained about 20 eggs.

The mother Maiasaura brought leaves and berries back to the nest for her babies to eat.

Ankylosaurus

Ankylosaurus had two heavy lumps of bone at the end of its tail. It could swing these at enemies like a huge hammer. Most of the time, this dinosaur was a peaceful plant eater.

Meat-eating dinosaurs like this Spinosaurus would have found Ankylosaurus a difficult meal to eat!

Ankylosaurus was protected by long spikes of bone on its head and shoulders.

Each lump of bone on the tail was as big as a basketball.

Bony tail
The tail club of *Ankylosaurus* was made of bones, which had become stuck together.

Pieces of bone as big as dinner plates protected the back of Ankylosaurus.

Triceratops

Triceratops was a peaceful plant eater, for most of the time. However, if an enemy came near, it charged with its head down, and jabbed with its long, sharp horns. The wide frill of bone over its neck made it look even more scary.

Like all dinosaurs, Triceratops had tough, scaly skin.

Triceratops had to protect itself from big meat eaters, like this Tyrannosaurus rex.

Triceratops used the long, sharp horns above its eyes to stab its enemies.

Shadow dino!

Put your fingers in the positions shown, between a desk lamp and the wall. See the shadowy Triceratops!

Stegosaurus

This dinosaur had tall, thin plates of bone on its back. They may have soaked up the heat from the Sun to warm the dinosaur up. The warmer *Stegosaurus* was, the faster it was able to move.

Stegosaurus had a mouth shaped like a bird's beak. It used this to peck at plants.

The back plates were as tall and wide as a pillow. They were only as thick as your wrist.

Tiny brain
Stegosaurus was as big as an elephant, but its brain was as small as your thumb. So it wasn't very clever!

The sharp, spiky tail was swung at enemies that came too near.

Deinonychus

Deinonychus hunted in packs. This way it could attack dinosaurs much bigger than itself, like this one-tonne *Tenontosaurus*. This would give it enough food for a whole week.

Deinonychus had strong back legs. It could run fast, jump high and leap a long way.

Clever dino?

The brain of Deinonychus was quite big compared to other dinosaurs. It may have been quite clever.

Deinonychus had a long, stiff tail to help it keep its balance.

A huge, curved claw was used to rip open the skin of victims.

Ornithomimus

Some dinosaurs, like *Ornithomimus*, were **fast runners.** *Ornithomimus* was an 'ostrich dinosaur'. It was very similar in size and shape to the bird of today, the ostrich. It could reach speeds of 80 kilometres an hour when running.

Ornithomimus had strong muscles in its hips and legs, to take long, quick strides.

The lower legs and feet were long, slim and light.

Ornithomimus had no teeth. Its mouth was was like a beak, pecking and snapping at leaves or lizards.

Fastest!
Ornithomimus could not run as fast as an ostrich, or the fastest runner today, the cheetah.

Parasaurolophus

The plant eater *Parasaurolophus* had a long tube of bone sticking up from the back of its head. The dinosaur may have blown air through this tube to make loud noises – just like an elephant does when it 'trumpets' through its trunk.

Parasaurolophus may have made noises to frighten off enemies or to find a mate.

Dino-song!
Roll a card sheet into a tube. Make noises through it. Maybe this was how Parasaurolophus sounded.

The skin was bumpy, as if it was covered in small pebbles. A long, pointy tail helped the dinosaur to balance.

Air was breathed in through the nose. It then passed through the hollow tube on the head, before going into the body.

Compsognathus

Compsognathus was the smallest dinosaur. Even though it was small, it was still fierce. It hunted little creatures such as insects, worms — and perhaps baby dinosaurs.

Compsognathus had small, sharp teeth for biting its tiny victims.

Spiky claws helped Compsognathus to grab its food.

This tiny dinosaur weighed only 3 kilograms – less than a pet cat.

Teeny dino!
Compsognathus was as big as a chicken, but much thinner and without the feathers.

Fun facts

Tyrannosaurus rex (tie-ran-oh-sore-us)
It means 'King of the tyrant lizards'

Brachiosaurus (brak-ee-oh-sore-us)
It means 'Arm lizard'

Maiasaura (my-ah-sore-ah)
It means 'Good mother lizard'

Ankylosaurus (an-ky-loh-sore-us)
It means 'Stiff or fused lizard'

Triceratops (tri-serra-tops)
It means 'Three horns on the face'

Stegosaurus (steg-oh-sore-us)
It means 'Roof lizard'

Deinonychus (die-non-i-kuss)
It means 'Terrible claw'

Ornithomimus (or-nee-tho-mee-mus)
It means 'Like an ostrich'

Parasaurolophus (para-sore-ol-off-us)
It means 'Beside ridged lizard'

Compsognathus (comp-sog-nath-us)
It means 'Elegant jaw'